SCHUMANN

MW00786200

SIX ETUDES IN CANON FORM, OPUS 56

Arranged for One Piano, Four Hands by Georges Bizet

EDITED BY MAURICE HINSON AND ALLISON NELSON

AN ALFRED MASTERWORK EDITION

Cover art: Ploughed Field, *c. 1830*
by Caspar David Friedrich (1774–1840)
Oil on Canvas
Hamburger Kunsthalle, Germany/
The Bridgeman Art Library

ROBERT SCHUMANN

Contents

Foreword 3

About the Music 4

About This Edition 5

Suggested Further Reading 5

Acknowledgements 5

SIX ETUDES IN CANON FORM, OP. 56

No. 1: *Pas trop vite* 6

No. 2: *Avec beaucoup d'expression* 12

No. 3: *Andantino—Un peu plus animé* 20

No. 4: *Espressivo—Un peu plus mouvementé* 24

No. 5: *Pas trop vite* 32

No. 6: *Adagio* 42

SIX ETUDES IN CANON FORM, Op. 56
Arranged for One Piano, Four Hands by Georges Bizet
Edited by Maurice Hinson and Allison Nelson

Foreword

In 1845, Robert Schumann (1810–1856) wrote three sets of pieces for the pedal piano: *Six Etudes in Canon Form*, Op. 56, *Four Sketches*, Op. 58 and *Six Fugues on the Name B-A-C-H*, Op. 60 (the latter being for organ or pedal piano). A pedal piano consists of a foot-pedal mechanism (pedalboard), similar to an organ. The pedalboard is generally used for basic harmonic support, and is designed to play the bass line of a composition, sometimes in octaves.

At the beginning of 1845, Schumann—together with his wife, Clara (1819–1896)—embarked on an intense course of contrapuntal studies. Robert Schumann's admiration for Bach and his absorption with the study of counterpoint led him to rent a pedalboard attachment for his home, inspiring him to write pieces specifically for pedal piano. It is possible that Robert's interest in Bach began with his first teacher, organist and choir director Johann Gottfried Kuntsch (1775–1855), to whom the *Six Etudes* are dedicated.

The great French composer Georges Bizet (1838–1875) arranged the *Six Etudes in Canon Form*, Op. 56 for one piano, four hands. These etudes are not simply technical finger exercises like Hanon or Czerny, but true works of art like the Chopin etudes. They make wonderful music while working the muscles of the hands and fingers. The canon is the strictest form of counterpoint, in which two or more voices present the same theme in overlapping succession. Imitation may begin on any note and can be any rhythmic distance from the initial theme.

The first Carnegie Hall performance of any of the Op. 56 etudes was on April 11, 1916, when Percy Grainger (1882–1961) performed Etude No. 3. The first complete performance of the six etudes at Carnegie Hall was on December 8, 1939, when Vitya Vronsky (1909–1992) and Victor Babin (1908–1972) performed Debussy's two-piano arrangement of the etudes. More recently, pianists Emanuel Ax (b. 1949) and Yefim Bronfman (b. 1958) performed the two-piano arrangement at the University of California, Berkeley on March 26, 2005.

About the Music

Editors' note: The use of pedal is recommended for the primo player; however, care should be taken not to cover up the imitation in the secondo part.

No. 1: Pas trop vite. 6

This fairly traditional-sounding canon uses baroque figuration. It is basically written in two voices, and the canon at the octave continues throughout the piece. The tonal center moves to the subdominant at measure 17, and transitional material brings back the opening subject at measure 25. The use of sixteenth notes slows in measure 37, and colorful harmonies lead to the final cadence. Good finger independence is required, as well as the clear execution of trills and scale passages in both hands.

No. 2: Avec beaucoup d'expression 12

This melodious, lyrical piece provides a strong contrast to the first canon. The graceful $\frac{12}{8}$ meter imparts a light, smooth motion. Canonic repetition is divided into two-measure groups, with the second measure sounding like an echo of the first measure. Colorful harmonic progressions are aided by non-harmonic tones and suspensions. Touch contrast (legato, staccato, non-legato) is required, as well as voice independence in the same hand.

No. 3: Andantino—Un peu plus animé 20

This melody and accompaniment with lovely harmonies suggest the style of Felix Mendelssohn's (1809–1847) Songs Without Words. The canon is heard at the fifth, every two beats. The second entrance suggests an echo. Careful shading and artistic legato are required throughout. The thicker secondo part must be adjusted to the thin sonorities of the primo part.

No. 4: Espressivo—Un peu plus mouvementé 24

The sixteenth notes should not be taken too fast, so that the melodious quality can come through easily. The canon is employed at the fifth. The piece is written in A–B–A form (A = measures 1–19; B = 20–43; A = 44–57; coda = 58–66) and juxtaposes sections of A-flat major with F minor. The canon is heard in the top two voices of the primo, while the secondo provides repeated chords for the accompaniment.

No. 5: Pas trop vite. 32

This canon is well camouflaged within the lively staccato chords, which makes it difficult to hear. The A–B–A form (A = measures 1–36; B = 37–82; A = 83–111) does not provide for much contrasting material. Some of the performance techniques required here are playing melodies embedded in staccato chords, a light touch, and performing within a restricted dynamic range.

No. 6: Adagio. 42

The sonorities of this canon suggest the sound of an organ. A–B–C form is used here (A = measures 1–17; B = 17–32; C = 33–54; coda = 54–66). The A and C sections sound rather homophonic. Imitation in all voices is found in the B section, which is a small fugue. Interesting chromaticism is found in the coda. Good legato is required, as well as finger independence and fine control of shadings.

About This Edition

All fingerings and parenthetical material is editorial. This edition is based on the Durand edition, Paris, France, no date.

Suggested Further Reading

Jensen, Eric Frederick. *Schumann*. Oxford University Press, 2001.

Maxwell, Carolyn and Devan, William. *Schumann Solo Piano Literature*. Boulder, CO, Maxwell Music Evaluation, 1984.

Ostwald, Peter. *Schumann: The Inner Voices of a Musical Genius*. Northeastern University Press, 1985.

Plantinga, Leon P. *Schumann as Critic*. New Haven and London, Yale University Press, 1967.

Taylor, Ronald. *Robert Schumann: His Life and Work*. New York, 1982.

Walker, Alan. ed. *Robert Schumann: The Man and His Music*. London, Barrie & Jenkins, 1972.

Acknowledgements

Thanks to editors E. L. Lancaster and Carol Matz for their generous assistance and expert editorial advice.

Six Etudes in Canon Form

Robert Schumann (1810–1856)
Op. 56

SECONDO

Six Etudes in Canon Form

Robert Schumann (1810–1856)
Op. 56

PRIMO

(a) In all six of these etudes, the use of pedal is recommended for the primo player;
however, care should be taken not to cover up the imitation in the secondo part.

SECONDO

SECONDO

(a) This RH melody continues in the LH of the primo part at measure 33.

PRIMO

SECONDO

(With great expression)
Avec beaucoup d'expression, ♩. = 60

2.

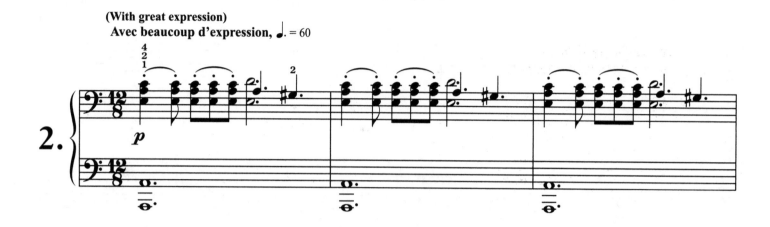

SECONDO

SECONDO

SECONDO

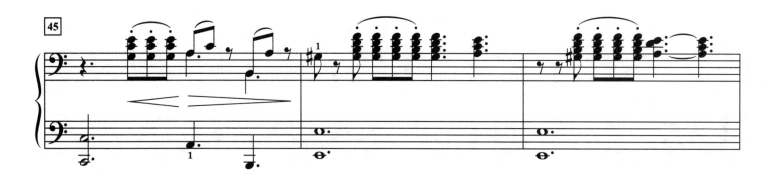

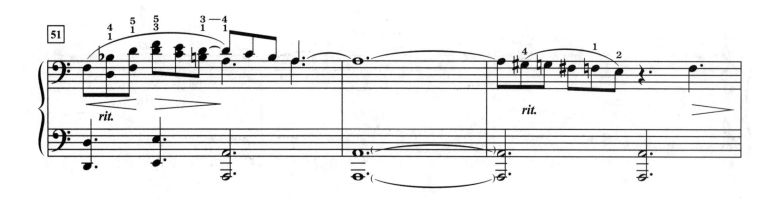

SECONDO

PRIMO

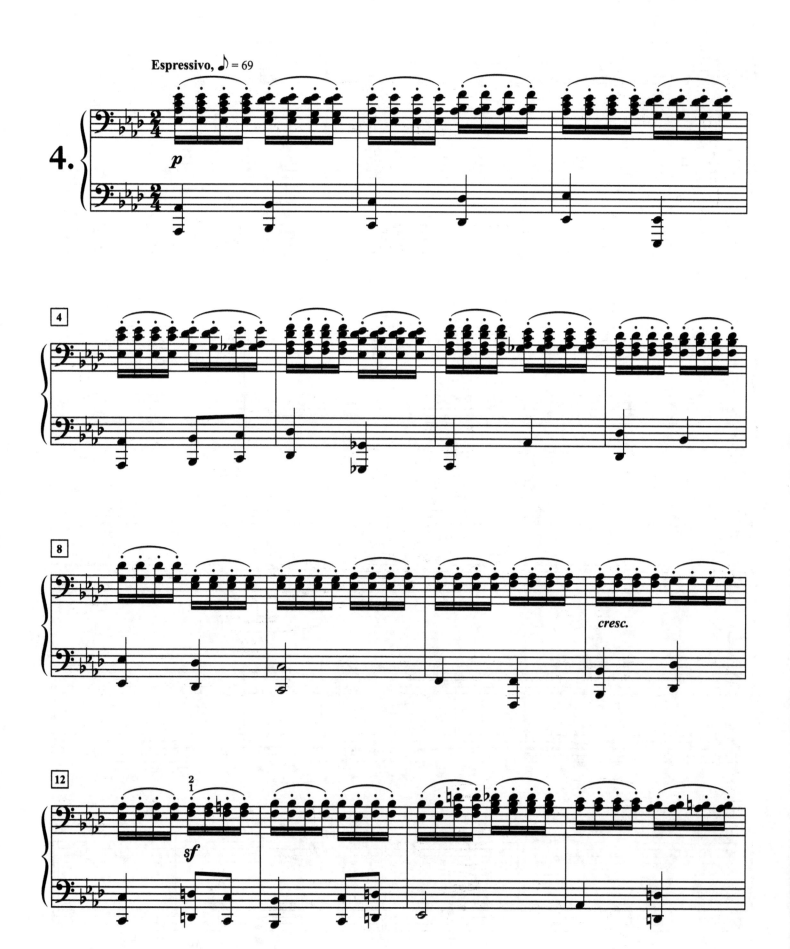

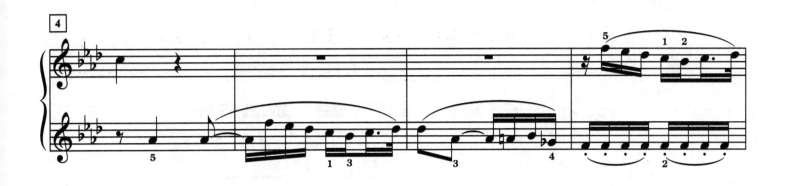

SECONDO

(A little faster)
Un peu plus mouvementé

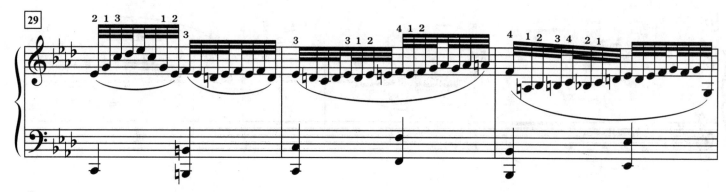

(a) In measures 25–29, the primo LH crosses over the secondo RH.

ⓐ In measures 25–29, the primo LH crosses over the secondo RH.

SECONDO

PRIMO

SECONDO

PRIMO

(a) This melody note ends the imitation of the phrase in measure 18 of the primo part.

SECONDO

SECONDO

ⓑ For ease of performance, the player could redistribute the alto and tenor voices between the hands.

SECONDO

6.

6.

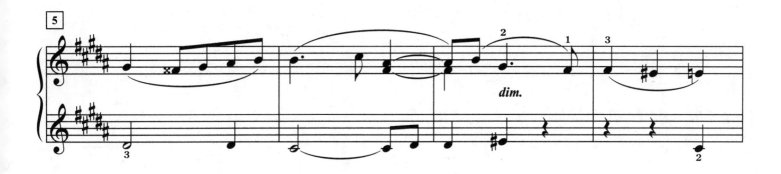

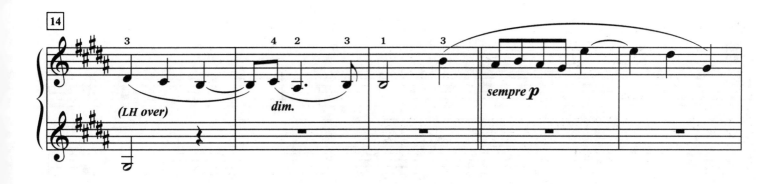

SECONDO

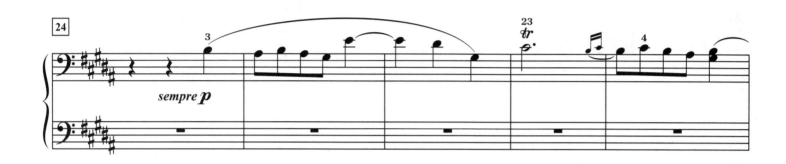

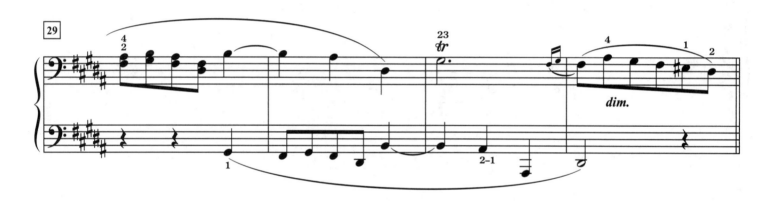

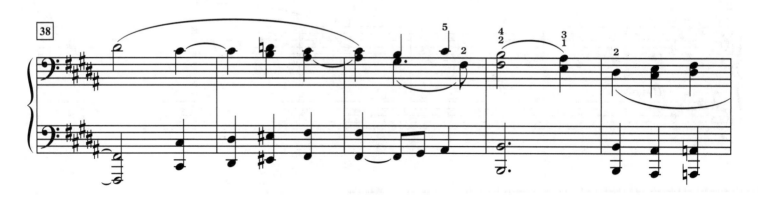

PRIMO